Autism Connections

More than Words

The Many Ways We Communicate

Leslie Kimmelman

Lerner Publications ◆ Minneapolis

Alongside friends from *Sesame Street*, children will explore how we all experience the world in unique ways—from developing friendships and flexible thinking to how we communicate and receive support. This series celebrates all children, helping young readers and their grown-ups appreciate the amazing qualities in everyone, fostering greater understanding.

Sincerely,
the Editors at Sesame Workshop

Table of Contents

Hello, Friends!

Hi! Hello! How are you doing? There are many different ways to say hello.

¡Hola, amigos!
That means "Hello, friends" in Spanish.

Many Ways to Communicate

There are also ways to communicate, or share information, without talking. You can use your body to say hello.

You can wave or give a high five.

You can communicate with your face too. How do you think each of these friends is feeling?

I smile when
I'm happy.

Some people use sign language to communicate. This sign means "I love you."

Me wonder how to say "cookie" in sign language.

Some people use their voice to talk. Others might use a special tablet, or "talker," to help them communicate.

This is my talker!

Listening is an important part of communication too.

Thanks for listening to my story, Bert!

We all have our own unique style of communicating. Sometimes we're loud, and sometimes we're quiet!

I love talking quietly to my friend Julia!

However we communicate, we all want to be understood. What will you tell your friends today?

Elmo loves you!

Happy Talk

How can you tell that each of these friends is happy? What is your favorite way to show that you feel happy?

Glossary

communicate: to share ideas with one another

sign language: a way of communicating that uses hands

talker: a tablet that a person can use to help them communicate

unique: special or the only one of its kind

Read More

Andrews, Elizabeth. *My Friend with Autism*. Cody Koala, 2024.

Davis, Raymie. *Feelings*. PowerKids Press, 2025.

Gabor, Nicole. *Sign Your ABCs with Sesame Street*. Lerner Publications, 2026.

Index

Photo Acknowledgments

Image credits: Kinzie Riehm/Getty Images, p. 4; SDI Productions/Getty Images, p. 6; Inti St Clair/Getty Images, p. 8 (left); pondsaksit/Getty Images, p. 8 (middle); LaylaBird/Getty Images, p. 8 (right); kwanchaichaiudom/Getty Images, p. 10; Arturo Peña Romano Medina/Getty Images, p. 12; LittleBee80/Getty Images, p. 14; kate_sept2004/Getty Images, p. 16; FatCamera/Getty Images, p. 18; Ariel Skelley/Getty Images, p. 20.

Lerner Publications Company
An imprint of Lerner Publishing Group, Inc.
241 First Avenue North
Minneapolis, MN 55401 USA

For reading levels and more information, look up this title at www.lernerbooks.com.

Main body text set in Mikado a.
Typeface provided by HvD Fonts.

Editor: Nicole Berglund **Designer:** Mary Ross **Photo Editor:** Nicole Berglund
Lerner team: Martha Kranes

Library of Congress Cataloging-in-Publication Data

Names: Kimmelman, Leslie author
Title: More than words : the many ways we communicate / Leslie Kimmelman.
Description: Minneapolis : Lerner Publications, [2026] | Series: Sesame Street autism connections | Includes bibliographical references and index. | Audience: Ages 4–8 | Audience: Grades K–1 | Summary: "There are many different ways of communicating! From facial expressions to tablets, readers explore alongside the Sesame Street characters all the ways we can connect with others"— Provided by publisher.
Identifiers: LCCN 2025011128 (print) | LCCN 2025011129 (ebook) | ISBN 9798765685105 library binding | ISBN 9798348029227 paperback | ISBN 9798765698303 epub
Subjects: LCSH: Communication—Juvenile literature
Classification: LCC HM1206 .K564 2026 (print) | LCC HM1206 (ebook) | DDC 302.2—dc23/eng/20250820

LC record available at https://lccn.loc.gov/2025011128
LC ebook record available at https://lccn.loc.gov/2025011129

Manufactured in the United States of America
1-1012743-54586-6/24/2025